Ornaments

Ornaments

Creating Handmade Tree Decorations

Carol Endler Sterbenz

**Andrews McMeel
Publishing**

Kansas City

Ornaments: Creating Handmade Tree Decorations copyright © 2000 by Carol Endler Sterbenz. Photographs copyright © 2000 by Richard Felber. All rights reserved. Printed in Italy. No part of this book may be used or reproduced in any manner whatsoever without written permission except in the case of reprints in the context of reviews. For information, write Andrews McMeel Publishing, an Andrews McMeel Universal company, 4520 Main Street, Kansas City, Missouri 64111.

Library of Congress Cataloging-in-Publication Data
Sterbenz, Carol Endler
  Ornaments : creating handmade tree decorations / Carol Endler Sterbenz.
    p. cm.
  Includes index.
  ISBN 0-7407-1023-0
  1. Christmas tree ornaments. I. Title.

TT900.C4 S7316 2000
745.594'12—dc21   00-038959

Every effort has been made to present the information in the book in a clear, complete, and accurate manner. It is important that all instructions are followed carefully, as failure to do so could result in injury. The authors, editors, and publisher or Andrews McMeel disclaim any and all liability resulting therefrom.

ATTENTION: SCHOOLS AND BUSINESSES

Andrews McMeel books are available at quantity discounts with bulk purchase for education, business, or sales promotional use. For information, please write to: Special Sales Department, Andrews McMeel Publishing, 4520 Main Street, Kansas City, Missouri 64111.

dedication

This book is dedicated with love to my husband,

John,

and his gentle and wise spirit.

acknowledgments

After many years of designing, I remain exhilarated by, and grateful for the opportunity to dwell in creative spaces for such extended periods of time as creating this collection of Christmas tree ornaments required. My immersion yielded as immense a satisfaction as any creative pursuit I have had. And just as fortunate, while I worked in the halo of my table light, a group of extremely talented people contributed their unique gifts and hard work so that my original vision would glow in the pages of this book. I want to especially thank:

The staff at Andrews McMeel Publishing, especially my editor, Jean Lowe, who responded to the ebb and flow of my creative efforts with wisdom and support, and who shaped the wonderful book you hold in your hands; and special recognition is also due to Stephanie Farley, Elizabeth Nuelle, Marti Petty, Erin Friedrich and Lisa Martin.

Richard Felber, whose beautiful photography gives life and allure to each and every exquisite detail of each of the ornaments; and to John Dee, his assistant, whose knowledgeable contributions made an important difference every time.

My daughters, especially Genevieve, whose sensitive styling created contexts that enhanced the intrinsic meaning, wit, and poetry of each of the ornaments; and to Gabrielle, who assisted with lithe and cheerful spirit.

And finally, my son, Rodney, whose honest feedback at the very beginning of this creative journey inspired me to find new levels of expression, resulting in a new dimension of ideas I would not have known otherwise.

Contents

introduction

*t*he tradition of decorating a tree is an ancient one, but for me it dates back to my childhood, when my sisters and I gathered in the kitchen with ribbons, buttons, beads and a host of ordinary stationery supplies strewn over the table so that we could make new ornaments to hang on the tree—pine cones hung by slender ribbons, woven heart baskets that would be filled with candy by Christmas morning, and cotton snowmen bundled in woolen scarves.

I continued the tradition of making ornaments through the years, especially with my own children. I look back with a great affection at the ornaments they made through their childhood years. Every Christmas we take out the ornaments, unwrap them, and hang them on our tree—molded figures of girls with jump ropes, superheroes with flowing capes, and curled shiny paper in the shape of doves. In an instant, time stands still as I re-experience the moments in our lives when my children made these ornaments, and I am grateful for these symbolic testimonies of their young hands and our family gatherings.

Our family has grown up and the children are all living in their own homes now, but the tradition of getting together to make handmade ornaments remains. I have learned a lot from our gatherings and from my work as a designer and editor. *Ornaments* represents my best work and I am happy to offer you this collection of original ornaments. Although I have no one favorite, because I appreciate the serendipity and skill that went into creating each one, I am certain of one common thread that ran through the process of making each ornament: I absolutely loved combining shiny findings and little tins to make the watches and clocks; I was enchanted when I found the exact emerald-cut rhinestones I needed to perfectly accent the red velvet slippers. And I was satisfied to discover that the simple etching method I used on larger decorative vases was exactly the same one I could use on the delicate glass balls; all I had to do was soak off the plastic coating that prevented my first attempts from being successful.

I know that it is in the sharing of the creative process, the serendipitous discoveries that congeal a design and the beauty of each little work that bring me back to making ornaments every year. I have been rewarded with inspiration at late hours; I have been accompanied on the path by my dearest friend and husband, John, and I have been taught new techniques by our children, Genevieve, Rodney, and Gabrielle. For it has been in their innocent and earnest work that I have found the secret joys of making ornaments for our tree. Simply, it is fun. And more so, it is in the very activity of making something by hand that we could all join in the creative process, each of us free to pursue the muse wherever it takes us, knowing that at the end of the road, we would have a concrete symbol of what I valued most—time with the people I love, celebrating one of the most meaningful holidays of the year.

When you page through this collection of ornaments, you will see original designs that were developed specifically for anyone who loves making beautiful decorations. The techniques are straightforward and easy, even though the directions appear long at times. I thought I would rather include explanations that alert you to the bends in the creative road than let you go off in the wrong direction, which isn't to say that your imagination will not play a vital and fulfilling role in your work. It only means that you will be given the basic technical model for each ornament from which you can unleash your own creative energies according to your own tastes and style. The materials used for all the ornaments are easy to find. I purposely and consistently used a set lexicon of materials throughout the book so that one shopping trip would yield all you need to make all the ornaments within these covers. Hence, red velvet pops up on the seat of the French café chair and the little shoes, and in the larger cornucopia project. I also used more wire than I have before, having found a new appreciation for its versatility and ease of use. Hence, I created chandeliers with bent-wire curlicues and teardrop crystals that rival those in Versailles. Well, maybe not entirely, but you will find a new pleasure in making the featured chandeliers. I suspect you will go off on your own and create more majestic lighting fixtures of your own invention.

For invention and fantasy play such a large role in the design of each ornament—both mine and yours. It is so clear to me that every ornament is actually a little fantasy, a replica of something you may actually see in comparatively larger, even immense, size or in a smaller size than in real life—cottages with glowing windows, jeweled snap peas and pears frozen in time in all their glittering splendor. Isn't that just the way designing should be, that each ornament should have meaning in our here and now, in our daily lives? I know that the objects that move me are those that inhabit my home and my thoughts, and now this collection. My sweet memories of France emanate from the chiming wall clock; my love of nature is echoed in the poised flight of the snowbird; and my love of whimsy flutters on the wings of the glitter butterflies, and the glass bugs made of beads. How else could I enter the world of dance than through the sight of the hand-beaded tutus with gossamer skirts, each seeming to float up in my imaginings of lighted stages and the strains of the symphony?

You will find that making ornaments is not only a tradition, it is a form of joyful prayer. I dedicate this collection to my family and all of you who recognize the soul's necessity to make something by hand, especially at Christmas, when the world is waiting for a miracle. And we can create such simple yet significant ones using our own hands.

CAROL ENDLER STERBENZ

Carol Endler Sterbenz

SEPTEMBER 2000

9

Striped Balls

*h*ere is one of the easiest and fastest ways to glamorize your ball ornaments whether they are new or old: Add stripes using super-shiny metallic tape. The tape is unfurled directly from the roll and pressed down on the surface of the ornament, creating wedge-shaped sections of varying sizes.

materials

red ball ornaments, 1¾" in diameter
silver metallic tape, ⅛" wide

you will also need

glass cleaner ✳ paper towels ✳ scissors

directions

1 prepare the ornament

Carefully remove the top cap from the ball by pinching the wire loop together with your fingers; ease the wire prongs out of the ball and set the cap aside; then, clean the ball with glass cleaner and paper towels.

2 decorate the ball

Peel a 1" length of tape from the roll. Hold the ball in one hand and the roll of tape in the other. Gently press the end of the tape to the center of the top neck of the ball; stretch and press the tape around the ball and back up to the neck on the opposite side, allowing the tape to extend by ¼" above the top of the neck. Then, cut the tape, pressing the extra tape inside the neck. Repeat the process to divide the ball into quarters, or as desired, adding more stripes in between those laid down to make narrower sections.

replace the cap

Replace the cap, being careful to squeeze the wire prongs together to ease them into the ball without breaking the neck of the ornament.

★

Designer's Tip: FOR A PRETTY VARIATION, MIX TAPES IN DIFFERENT COLORS AND DIFFERENT WIDTHS TO CREATE THE WEDGE-SHAPED DESIGN ON ONE ORNAMENT.

Chandelier Crystal Wreath

What more dazzling new use for old chandelier crystals can there be than these little wreaths? Made by stringing beads and crystals onto a wire and bending the strand into a hoop, these wreaths are the perfect decorative accent for your tree and for any wrapped gift.

materials for wreath with floral crystals

8 crystals in floral shape, each ⅞" in diameter
40 clear crystal beads with silver linings, each 4 mm
24-gauge spool wire in silver finish
Finished size: 3⅛" diameter

materials for wreath with faceted crystals

10 faceted chandelier crystals, each ⅝" wide
50 clear crystal beads with silver linings, each 4mm
24-gauge spool wire in silver finish
Finished size: 3" diameter

you will also need

glass cleaner ✳ paper towels
round-nose pliers ✳ junky scissors

directions for both wreaths

prepare the crystals

1

Remove any existing wires from the chandelier crystals, making certain there is one clear hole through which you can insert a wire; then, clean the crystals with glass cleaner and paper towels.

string the beads and the crystals

2

Unroll and cut a 14" length of wire from the spool. Insert one end of the wire into a hole in one crystal and slide the crystal down the wire 3"; twist the crystal twice in place so that the front of the crystal faces front, leaving the 3" tail free. Insert the opposite end of the wire into five clear beads, sliding them down to meet the crystal; repeat the process until all the crystals are strung.

shape the wreath

3

Form a rough hoop shape with the strand of beads and crystals. Thread the end of wire back through the first five-bead section, exiting out one bead and pulling the wire taut to secure the join; clip off the extra wire. Thread the short 3" tail of wire back into the adjacent five-bead section, exiting out one bead; then, clip off the extra wire.

finish the wreath

4

Lay the wreath on a flat surface and use your fingers to shape a circle from inside the hoop shape.

Designer's Tip: ADD BOWS MADE FROM STRANDS OF RED BEADS OR MIX DIFFERENT TYPES AND SHAPES OF CRYSTALS ON ONE WREATH.

Jeweled Snap Peas

*l*ittle will rival the exquisite beauty of this jeweled ornament on your tree. Comprised of sparkling rhinestones glued to ordinary (but heavy-gauge) aluminum foil, this snap pea is filled with plump peas made of clear glass beads.

materials

36-gauge aluminum foil ✳ transparent green
glass paint ✳ beads: 4 clear green glass beads,
each 16mm ✳ 2 pearls, each 4mm ✳ assorted rhinestones:
14 light green, each 8mm ✳ 10 turquoise, each 6mm
70 assorted colors, each 4mm ✳ 7" length of
medium-gauge armature wire

you will also need

pencil ✳ scissors: straight blade and manicure ✳ tweezers
pliers ✳ soft cloth ✳ paintbrush ✳ gold spray paint
five-minute epoxy glue ✳ toothpicks ✳ plastic lid

directions

trace and cut out the patterns

1

Photocopy the patterns for two pods, stem leaves and two single leaves on page 120; rough-cut them out ½" beyond the marked line all around and then cut out the pattern pieces along the marked lines. On a flat work surface, unfurl a 12" long sheet from the roll of foil, flattening the section with a soft cloth. Lay one pod, stem leaves, and two leaf pattern pieces on the foil, using short lengths of tape to secure them in place. Use a sharp pencil and light pressure to trace along the dash line on the leaf so that the foil indents slightly; use scissors to crudely cut out the pieces from foil. Then, use manicure scissors to accurately cut around each pattern piece along the heavy outside line. Remove the paper patterns from the foil.

2 *paint the pieces*

On a protected surface, apply an even coat of glass paint to one side of the foil pod section and to both sides of the foil leaves, curling the edges of the foil to prevent the foil from laying flat. Let the paint dry. Lay the pod section, unpainted side up, on a work surface. Spray on two light coats of gold paint, allowing paint to dry between coats. To make the tendrils, cut armature into two uneven lengths; use pliers to make a small hook in one end of each length. Apply an even coat of green paint to all surfaces; then, hang up the wires by their hooks to dry.

3 *shape and assemble the pod and tendril*

Gently shape the pod into a wide, soft U. Following the manufacturer's directions, prepare a small blob of epoxy glue. Apply glue to one end of a tendril; then, lay it in the dash-lined stem section, folding the foil around the wire to secure it. Let the glue dry. Position and glue the stem leaf section over the fold, then glue single leaf anywhere on remaining tendril. Twist tendrils together at ends.

4 *lay out the jewel pattern*

On the second copy of the pod pattern, arrange the rhinestones, mixing the sizes and colors as desired. **Note:** Arrange the smallest rhinestones in a broad band at the curve of the snap pea for best adhesion; when satisfied, follow the manufacturer's directions and mix up one small batch of five-minute epoxy.

decorate the pod

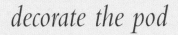

Note: Once the glue dries, the rhinestones cannot be moved. Following the arrangement of rhinestones on the paper pattern, lift up one rhinestone at a time, using tweezers if necessary; mix epoxy glue in plastic lid and use toothpick to apply epoxy glue to the flat back. Immediately lay it in the position on the foil that correlates to the paper pattern. Repeat the process of lifting, gluing, and pressing the rhinestones to the surface of the pod until it is decorated. To finish, use pliers to gently crimp along the edge of the pod, roughly following the indentation formed in Step 1.

add the peas

Use five-minute epoxy to secure one pearl, four glass beads, and another pearl in a line inside the U of the pod; then glue the remaining leaf to the remaining tendril in any position. Twist the tendril around the tendril at the stem, as desired.

Designer's Tip: MAKE SEVERAL PLAIN SNAP PEAS, PAINTING EACH A SHADE OF GREEN; USE ALL PEARLS INSTEAD OF GLASS BEADS FOR THE PEAS.

Old-Fashioned Tinsel

*C*onstructed like the tinsel of the 1940s, these icicles are easy to make using heavy-gauge aluminum foil and permanent markers. All you do is glue two sheets of foil together, draw stripes on one side of the foil, cut into strips and twist them into icicles.

materials

36-gauge aluminum foil ✳ permanent markers:
Nile green, deep magenta, cobalt blue, aquamarine
Finished size: ⅜" wide x 8½" long
Yield: two dozen ornaments

you will also need

soft cloth ✳ denatured alcohol ✳ paper towels
spray adhesive ✳ X-Acto knife ✳ straight-edge ruler
"T" pin ✳ spool filament thread

directions

cut the foil

1

On a protected work surface, unroll 2' of foil, smoothing the surface of the foil flat with a soft cloth. Run the blade of the X-Acto knife across the width of the foil to rough-cut off a 10" long section; repeat the process for a second 10" length of foil.

2 *laminate the foil*

Work in a well-ventilated room. Follow manufacturer's directions on the can of spray adhesive. Lay the foil sections on a very smooth, protected work surface. Use denatured alcohol and a paper towel to clean the foil. Apply a coat of adhesive to one side of each foil section; allow the glue to dry. Laminate the foil by laying the sections together, glued sides touching, straight edges even; smooth the surface with a soft cloth. Trim the ragged edge off the laminated foil so that you have a neat 8½" by 12" rectangle.

3 *mark the stripes*

Lay the laminated foil vertically on a very smooth, flat surface; use markers to draw vertical lines on the foil, spacing them as desired and switching colors as desired. Repeat the process until the entire sheet is striped. Let the ink dry.

4 *cut the foil strips*

Turn the marked foil so that the stripes run horizontally. Lay the straight-edge ruler ⅜" from the right edge of the foil, positioned so that it is perpendicular to the stripes. Run the blade of the X-Acto knife along the ruler to score a thin line, then go back and use firm pressure to cut through the foil. Set the cut strip aside. Repeat the process to form ⅜"-wide stripes until the foil is used up.

twist the strips

5

Holding the opposite ends of one foil strip in the fingers of both hands, pull the strip taut while twisting the ends in opposite directions. Continue twisting the foil until the entire strip is a gentle helix shape. Repeat the process with the remaining strips.

hang the tinsel

6

Use a "T" pin to puncture a hole in one end of the strip. Insert one end of a 6" length of filament in the hole, tying the ends together to secure; repeat the process for the remaining icicles.

Designer's Tip: APPLY GLUE TO ONE SIDE OF THE FOIL STRIP AND SPRINKLE ON MICRO-GLITTER INSTEAD OF MARKING ON STRIPES.

Time Capsule Timepieces

*t*his assortment of clocks and watches is so detailed, you may even strain to hear the sound of ticking! But as detailed as these timepieces appear, each began as an empty ointment tin. The added surprise is that each tin becomes a time capsule when a narrow band of paper is inscribed and hidden inside. To make any one of these classics, paint a lidded tin gold and glue on an assortment of jewelry findings and brass charms, using epoxy glue. Use your imagination to enhance the basic model described below. For example, add a pair of bell shaped findings for an alarm clock, a chain for a pocket watch, and cherubs and hoops for a French-styled wall clock.

materials

For the basic clock: 1½ ounce tin with lid,
1½" in diameter by ½" deep
For clock hands: two 2½" long eye pins in gold
For clock face: one ⁷⁄₁₆" diameter clock face charm
For winder: hoop side of toggle clasp
sheet of white paper
Finished size: 1½" wide by 2⅛" high by ½" deep

you will also need

denatured alcohol ✳ paper towels ✳ awl ✳ utility knife
plastic lid ✳ toothpicks ✳ five-minute epoxy glue
high tack glue ✳ scissors straight-edge ruler ✳ fine-line pen

directions

paint the tin

1 Work in a well-ventilated room. Remove the top lid from the bottom. Use alcohol and paper towels to clean all the surfaces of any grease or soil. Lay the sections on a protected work surface. Spray-paint one side of each section gold. Turn them to paint the opposite side; let the paint dry.

add the clock details

2 **For the winder:** Turn the tin bottom to its side and rest the rim on a broomstick or other round object; use an awl to puncture a hole ⅛" from the bottom edge. Carefully insert the tip of the utility knife into the hole and rock it gently to cut a ³⁄₁₆" slit. Insert the small loop side of the toggle hoop into the slit. Carefully follow the manufacturer's directions to mix up a batch of five-minute epoxy, then secure the hoop to the tin, using a dab of glue. Let the glue cure.

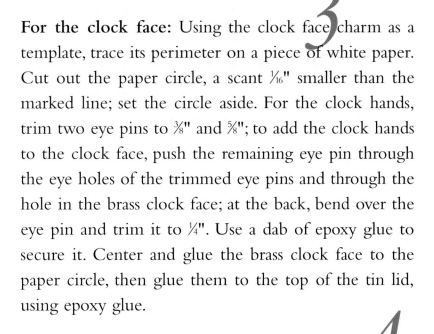

For the clock face: Using the clock face charm as a template, trace its perimeter on a piece of white paper. Cut out the paper circle, a scant ¹⁄₁₆" smaller than the marked line; set the circle aside. For the clock hands, trim two eye pins to ⅜" and ⅝"; to add the clock hands to the clock face, push the remaining eye pin through the eye holes of the trimmed eye pins and through the hole in the brass clock face; at the back, bend over the eye pin and trim it to ¼". Use a dab of epoxy glue to secure it. Center and glue the brass clock face to the paper circle, then glue them to the top of the tin lid, using epoxy glue.

For the message band: Cut a ½" by 11" strip from the white paper. Inscribe your personal message. Roll up the strip and place it in tin bottom. For longer messages, neatly glue several paper segments together in a long banner; notch the ends.

Designer's Tip: Photocopy any clock face from a home catalog, sizing it to fit the tin lid. To glamorize your clock, add rhinestones to the clock hands.

Ballet Tutus

*t*he ethereal layers of tulle and the fine silk in these miniature tutus make it easy to imagine the dancers in a corps de ballet. Using only a short length of silk ribbon for the bodice and a few circles of fine tulle, you can fashion a tutu worthy of any prima ballerina. Constructing the tutu requires only the most elementary sewing skills.

materials

For the bodice with straps:
12½" wire-edged ribbon, 2" wide ✳ 4½" satin ribbon,
⅛" wide ✳ matching thread ✳ fabric glue
For the bodice decoration: seed beads in gold
or colors, as desired ✳ beading needle
stem of ¼" wide artificial flowers
For the skirt: white tulle: 6 precut 8½" circles
Optional: ⅓ yd. satin ribbon in cream,
each approximately ¼" wide for ribbon sash

you will also need

straight pins ✳ ruler ✳ pencil
scissors ✳ sewing machine

directions

prepare the tulle for the skirt

1

Lay six circles together, all edges even; fold the circles in quarters, securing the folds using straight pins. Beginning at the point of the fold, measure and mark an arc 1½" from the point, using a ruler and a pencil. Cut along the marked arc. Remove the pins and open up the stack of circles. **Note:** You will have lifesaver-shaped rings. Secure the flat layers of tulle using straight pins. Make a straight cut from the outer edge of the ring (hem) to the inner edge of the ring (waistband), using scissors.

make the skirt

2 Position and pin one two-ring section together, all edges even; repeat the process to make two more two-ring sections. Use a double-threaded needle to sew a basting stitch around the waistband of each two-ring section, ¼" from the edge. Pull the tulle along the thread until the waistband measures about 5½". Set the section aside. Repeat the process to make two more gathered skirt sections. Layer and pin the three gathered skirt sections together along their waistbands, raw edges even. Machine-stitch the skirt sections together, a scant ¼" from the raw edges; set the skirt aside.

pleat the bodice front section

3 Measure and cut two lengths of ribbon, one 6" long and a second 6½" long. Fold the longer ribbon in half width-wise; then, machine-stitch the fold a scant ⅟₁₆" from the edge. Fold and stitch two more pin pleats, each ¼" from the center pleat, adding more pleats if necessary, until the ribbon measures 6".

attach skirt section to pin-pleated bodice

4 Lay the ribbon section and the gathered skirt section together, and pin waistband and the wire edge of ribbon even. Distribute the gathers of the skirt evenly across the ribbon, allowing ¼" length of ribbon free at each end. Machine-stitch the skirt to the bodice section, a scant ¼" from the edge.

make the straps

5

Cut the ⅛" wide ribbon in half; glue one length on each pin pleat opposite the center pin pleat, raw edges even. Let the glue dry.

make the bodice

6

Lay the second ribbon bodice section over the pleated bodice front, right sides together, all edges even. Machine-stitch the two short sides, a scant ¼" from the edge, and one long side at the top, ⅛" from the edge, trapping the straps in place. Turn the bodice to the right side.

decorate the bodice

7

Use a threaded beading needle to affix beads and blooms to the front, back, and straps of the bodice, in positions, as desired.

finish the tutu

8

Turn the tutu to the back and turn under the bottom edge of the ribbon a scant ¼". Use a threaded hand-sewing needle to secure. For each strap, tie a single knot at the end of each ribbon; then, tack the knot to the bodice back, ¼" from the edge. Overlap and tack back closed; add a ribbon sash, as desired.

✳

Designer's Tip: FOLLOWING THE MANUFACTURER'S DIRECTIONS, COLOR THE TULLE SKIRT TO COORDINATE WITH THE DRESS BODICE, USING COLD-WATER DYE.

Velvet Slippers

*i*t is easy to imagine the joyful fantasy of being able to fit your feet inside these glamorous slippers and dance straight into a Christmas fairy tale. You can make your own pair in a tiny size, and decorate them with rhinestones, or you can add a simple ribbon bow instead.

materials

scraps of red velvet * 2-ply chipboard
red construction paper * 4 square rhinestones
2½" long sections wooden dowel (½" diameter)
red acrylic paint

you will also need

scissors * craft paper * "T" pin * high-tack glue
hot-glue gun * glue sticks * paint brush

directions

prepare the patterns pieces

1

See the pattern on page 118. Use a copy machine to copy four pattern pieces for the shoe, shoe top, shoe-top lining, insole, and outer sole. Cut out the pattern pieces along the heavy line, using scissors.

cut out the shoe sections

2

Lay the pattern pieces for the shoe top, insole, and outer soles on chipboard. Trace all around the patterns. Cut out the chipboard sections. Lay the pattern piece for the shoe-top lining and the shoe-top outer sole on red construction paper; trace all around the patterns. Cut out the shoe lining along marked line; cut out the outersole ½" beyond marked line.

3 laminate the shoe sections

Lay the scraps of velvet on a protected work surface, a rough 5" square for the shoetop and 4½" by 3" for the insole, both pieces wrong side up. Lay the chipboard top shoe section on the craft paper. Brush the chipboard, including edges, with high-tack glue. Lay the shoetop section, glue side down, on the velvet, allowing at least ¼" all around; smooth the velvet flat. Trim the excess velvet to ¼" from all the edges. On one straight edge (without dash line) at the back of the shoe, trim the velvet even with the board. Notch the velvet around the curves. For the insole, apply a light coat of high-tack glue to the right side of the chipboard insole section. Press the insole section glue side down on the rectangle of velvet, gently smoothing the velvet in place. Trim the velvet to within ¼" of the chipboard.

4 glue the velvet to the chipboard

Brush high-tack glue onto the wrong side of the velvet allowances notched around the curves of the shoetop and insole sections. Fold and press down the velvet onto the board on both sections; repeat the process to glue and fold the allowance at the straight edge at the back of the shoe section. Let the glue dry.

5 glue the lining

Glue the lining to the outersole section. Apply light coat of glue to one side of chipboard outer sole. Press glue-side-down on center of paper lining. Clip curves and fold paper over to wrong side of chipboard, gluing in place.

shape the shoe

Use your hands to roll the toe section of the shoe until it holds its shape. Glue the overlapped section of the heel over the straight edge section; then secure the overlap, using "T" pins. Let the glue dry.

glue in the lining

Brush high-tack glue on the wrong side of the topshoe lining; slip it into the shoe, pressing it to the wrong side of the shoe, concealing the overlap at the heel and the raw edges of velvet.

install and glue the insole

Insert the insole into the shoe, velvet side up. Turn over the shoe and glue the allowances to the wrong side of the insole. Let the glue dry. Brush high-tack glue on the wrong side of the sole, then press it to bottom of the shoe.

affix the heels and rhinestones

Paint and secure heels. Apply coat of paint to each dowel section; let dry. Use hot-glue to affix one dowel to heel section (as indicated by red dash line on pattern). Affix rhinestones as shown.

Designer's Tip: INSTEAD OF VELVET, USE A PLAID SILK IN PINK AND GREEN FOR THE SHOE, AND ADD TINY FLOWERS IN A CRESCENT SHAPE AT THE TOE.

Etched Glass Balls

*t*here is nothing more elegant than the look of frosted pinstripes on a clear glass ball ornament. You can lay down patterns of every description on a glass ball of any size—from parallel stripes around the equator of a ball to softly swirling bands that are reminiscent of the sophisticated graphic patterns of the 1940s.

materials

plain glass balls ✴ pinstripe tape, ⅛" wide
glass-etching cream

you will also need

glass cleaner ✴ paper towels ✴ plastic drinking straw
masking tape ✴ scissors ✴ teaspoon ✴ craft paper
protective eyeware ✴ rubber gloves ✴ soft paintbrush

directions

prepare the ornament for etching

1

Carefully remove the top cap from the ball by pinching the wire loop together with your fingers; ease the wire prongs out of the ball and set the cap aside. To remove the plastic coating, soak the ball in warm water, gently rubbing the coating off, using the pads of your fingers; empty the ball of any water. Clean the ball with glass cleaner and paper towels. For a temporary handle, insert a straw to the neck opening, allowing it to rest on the bottom, and tape around the straw and the neck of the ball.

2   *lay down the masks in a pattern*

For the horizontal striped band, peel a 1" length of tape from the roll. Hold the ball in one hand and the roll of tape in the other. Press the end of the tape to any point on the equator of the ball. Pull and press down the tape around the circumference of the ball, stretching it slightly. Overlap the ends. Cut the tape; use the bowl side of a teaspoon to press down the edges of the tape. Repeat the process to add four additional strips of tape parallel to the first, two above and two below, leaving a scant ¼" between strips.

For the swirl pattern, peel a 1" length of tape from the roll; hold the ball in one hand and the roll of tape in the other. Align and press down the straight end of the tape to the top edge of the neck. Pull the tape from the roll, stretching it slightly to accommodate the curve of the ball, as you turn the ball slightly. Press the tape down, ending it underneath the ball directly over the cap. Cut the tape. Repeat the process to lay down more bands of tape a scant ¼" from the one previously laid or at wider intervals, as desired.

For the quadrant pattern with stars, peel a 1" length of tape from the roll. Hold the ball in one hand and the roll of tape in the other. Press the end of the tape to any point on the equator of the ball. Wrap the pinstripe tape around the ball, overlapping the tape at the end. Cut the tape. Use the bowl side of a teaspoon to press down the edges of the tape. Repeat the process to lay a second strip of tape perpendicular to the first strip. Press the stars to the center of two diagonal quadrants.

frost the pattern on the glass

Work in a well-ventilated area near a sink covered with craft paper; pull on gloves and hold the ball by the straw handle; use a paint brush to apply a ¹⁄₁₆" thick coat of etching cream over the surface of the ball, staying within the taped area. Allow the cream to remain on the glass for eight minutes, then wash off the cream under softly running water. Peel off the tape, then remove any cream residue using glass cleaner and towels. Replace the cap, being careful to squeeze the wire prongs together in order to ease them into the ball without breaking the neck.

Designer's Tip: COMBINE THE LOOK OF FROSTED STARS AND METALLIC STARS IN ONE QUADRANT, BY PASTING ON GOLD STATIONERY STARS AFTER THE ORNAMENT HAS BEEN ETCHED. OR, TO COLOR THE ORNAMENT, POUR ACRYLIC PAINT IN A CHOSEN COLOR INTO THE ORNAMENT, SWIRLING IT AROUND TO COAT THE INTERIOR OF THE BALL; THEN INVERT THE BALL OVER A CUP AND ALLOW THE EXCESS PAINT TO DRAIN OUT. RECAP THE ORNAMENT AND HANG.

✱ Charm Wreaths

*t*he beauty of these wreaths is that you can create sentimental mementos that symbolize the meaning of your holiday traditions using brass charms. The array of charms depicting themes like childhood toys, hobbies and sports, as well as simple shapes like hearts and stars is vast. To make a wreath, select an assortment of brass charms that represent one theme, and glue them to a metal hoop. You can also glue the charms to one another in a circle shape. Since the wreaths are reversible, you will have twice the fun of arranging these miniatures.

materials for toys of childhood

assortment of 20 to 24 brass charms, as desired
metal hoop with 2¼" diameter
Finished size: 3" diameter

you will also need

five-minute epoxy glue ✱ Fun Tack™ putty
plastic lids ✱ toothpicks

directions

prepare the charms

1

Use wire cutters to remove any loops for stringing, if desired.

arrange the charms

2

Arrange eight to ten charms on the hoop, mixing charms of different sizes, shapes, and finishes to achieve the greatest visual interest. Use gobs of Fun Tack™ placed under the charms to level them, if necessary. For the reverse side, use the hoop as a size guide, and arrange the remaining charms in a circle on the work surface.

glue on the charms

3

Mix up a small batch of five-minute epoxy glue in plastic lid, carefully following the manufacturer's directions; with a clock as orientation, use toothpick to apply glue on the hoop at the 12 noon position, leveling the charm with Fun Tack™, as needed. Repeat the process to affix three more charms, one each at 3, 6, and 9 o'clock. Repeat the process, gluing on more charms in the bare spaces or on a second level on the wreath. Wait ten minutes; then, repeat the process to affix the charms arranged for the second wreath on the reverse side of the hoop.

variations

The following wreaths do not require a metal hoop. The brass charms are arranged as before, and then glued to each other, using five-minute epoxy.

materials

For Victorian Scallop with Roses and Ribbon Bow Charms: scallop wreath with 2⅛" diameter ✶ arch of roses, about 1⅞" long ribbon bow, about 1¼" wide by 1¼" long
Finished size: 2⅛"

For Grape Vine with Ribbon Bow Accented with Rhinestone Charms: 8 grape vine branches 2¼" long ✶ ribbon bow 1⅜" wide by ¾" long copper rhinestone, 4mm
Finished size: 3½" diameter

Designer's Tip: Use high-gloss enamel to color the charms, using vials of paint designed for airplane model making.

Paper Pine Trees

*i*t is hard to believe that these majestic trees are made of the most ordinary materials—translucent vellum paper and painted sticks. A straightforward cutting process yields delicate tiers of intricately cut paper boughs which are then stacked on a wooden skewer to create the realistic-looking conifer. When the trees are "planted" near the lights on a Christmas tree, they create the look of a pine forest on a snowy winter's night.

materials

3 sheets of vellum, each 8½" square ✻ wooden skewer
Finished Size: 6½" high

you will also need

scissors: straight blade, manicure, and junky
pencil ✻ "T" pin ✻ stapler ✻ white acrylic paint
watercolor brush ✻ high-tack glue

directions

1 *prepare the patterns*

Trace the pattern for the small and large tiers of branches on page 116.

prepare the vellum and trace the patterns

2

Cut the sheets of vellum into rough quarters. Lay them in three stacks of four squares of paper each. Staple one corner of each stack to secure it. Lay the pattern for the small tier under the first square of one stack and trace the pattern. Lay the pattern for the large tier under the first square of the remaining two stacks and trace the pattern.

3 *cut out the tree boughs*

Use scissors, as appropriate, to cut along the marked lines of the traced pattern on each stack. Use a "T" pin to make a pilot hole in the middle of each tier. Stack the tiers on your work surface, ending with the stack of small tier of branches.

4 *trim and paint the skewer*

Use junky scissors to trim the blunt end of the skewer until it measures 6½". Paint the skewer white; let the paint dry.

shape the tiers

5

Use your fingers to make a crease in the middle of each branch, making certain all creases are made from the same side of the paper. **Note:** Paper will form irregular V shape.

assemble the tree

6

Insert the point of the skewer into the pilot hole of one tier; beginning with the large size, slide the tier down to within 1¾" of the trimmed end. Repeat the process, inserting and sliding eleven more tiers along the skewer, (ending with the small tiers) distributing the branches to resemble a live tree. To secure each tier, use the paintbrush to apply a dab of glue to the skewer; then, let the glue dry.

Designer's Tip: USE A COPIER TO REDUCE OR ENLARGE THE PATTERN TO MAKE VERY SMALL TREES THAT CAN STAND IN A FOAM-FILLED FLOWER POT AT EACH HOLIDAY PLACESETTING, OR TO MAKE VERY LARGE TREES FOR USE AS A TABLE CENTERPIECE. FOR THE CENTERPIECE, INSERT THE STEMS OF THE TREES INTO A LOG OF STYROFOAM, THEN CONCEAL IT WITH FAKE SNOW.

Hinged Scallop Shells

*b*each shells collected as souvenirs no longer need to be tucked away in a drawer. Instead, enjoy the memories of a sunny vacation during the winter holidays by transforming your shells into hinged boxes with gilded interiors. Five-minute epoxy glue is the secret to creating a durable hinge and a flawless finish.

materials

2 2" wide scallop shells ✶ gold spray paint
white acrylic paint, high gloss ✶ gold paint marker
6" length of blue satin ribbon, ⅛" wide
five-minute epoxy glue ✶ epoxy sealer
for decoration: two 14mm pearls and one star charm
Finished size: 2¼" high by 2" wide

you will also need

tile cutter ✶ 220-grit emery paper ✶ 2 bristle brushes
water color paintbrush ✶ toothpicks ✶ plastic lid

directions

prepare the shells

1 Line up the straight edges of the shells; if one is longer than the other, carefully use the tile cutter to "nibble" away the excess on the longer edge. Use emery paper dampened with water to smooth the exterior of each shell, making certain any rough surfaces and sharp edges are smoothed flat.

seal the shells

2 Work in a well-ventilated room. Follow the manufacturer's directions on the epoxy sealer and apply a thin coat to all surfaces of the shells, using a bristle brush. Let the sealer dry overnight until hard.

paint the shells

3 Paint the exterior of each shell white; repeat the process for a second coat. Let the paint dry. Place the shells, inside bowl-side facing up, on a protected work surface. Apply an even coat of gold paint to each bowl; repeat the process for a second coat. Let the paint dry thoroughly. Apply a final thin coat of epoxy sealer to all the surfaces of each shell; let the sealer dry overnight.

hinge the shells

4

Following the manufacturer's directions, mix up the five-minute epoxy glue on a plastic lid, using a toothpick. Apply a narrow line of glue to the straight edge of each shell; lay one end of the ribbon along the edge of one shell; then tilt the shells at a 75-degree angle. Press the glued edges together to form a tight bond, adding more epoxy, if necessary. Let the glue dry for ten minutes.

decorate the shells

5

Mix up a small amount of five-minute epoxy in a lid. Use a toothpick to apply three dabs of glue to the interior of one shell. Lay two pearls and one gold star on dabs of glue to affix the decorations. Use the gold paint marker to draw a border around the shells on the painted side.

Designer's Tip: APPLY A DÉCOUPAGE IMAGE TO THE INTERIOR OF ONE OF THE SHELLS. STEEL-ETCHED ENGRAVINGS OF WINTER SCENES ARE ESPECIALLY BEAUTIFUL.

Beaded Apple Halves

*t*he glamour of a retro-style beaded apple turns surprisingly witty when the apple is sliced in half and its interior is decorated with seed beads. The beading process is time-consuming but extraordinarily easy to do: Pin clear red beads to the exterior of the apple halves, then glue a layer of pearlized beads to their interiors.

materials

2" to 2½" wide foam apple ✳ 2 leaves
2 mm beads: 900 red (about 450 for each apple half)
20 gold (about 10 for the apple seeds on each apple half)
seed beads: 6 to 8 strands in pearlized white
900 straight pins, 1 cm long

you will also need

sharp knife ✳ 20-gauge galvanized steel wire
wire cutters ✳ round-nose pliers ✳ box lid
high-tack glue ✳ watercolor paint brush ✳ kitchen knife

directions

prepare the apple

1 Use a knife to cut the foam apple in half from the top stem to bottom core, using a steady sawing action for a clean cut. Set the halves aside. For hangers, cut two 3" lengths of wire, using the wire cutters. Use the pliers to bend one end into a tiny hook. Push the opposite end of the wire into the bottom core of one apple half, exiting out the top stem area. Use the pliers to bend the top wire into a hook. Repeat the process with the second apple half.

decorate the exterior skin of the apple

2 Position one red bead, hole side up, on the red rim of the apple. Push a pin through the hole in the bead and into the foam to secure it. Repeat the process, positioning and pinning beads to the apple skin close together to establish the rim. Continue beading the apple until the entire outside surface is covered.

decorate the sliced side of the apple

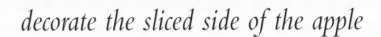

3

Hold the strands of seed beads over an inverted box lid. Cut the threads, allowing the beads to collect in the lid. Use a brush to apply a scant ⅟₁₆" thick coat of glue to the flat sliced foam. Use a spoon to scoop and pour white seed beads directly onto the glue, patting the beads flat with a kitchen knife. Position single gold beads in a crescent pattern to simulate apple seeds, adding scant dabs of glue as necessary to secure them. Repeat the process to decorate the other half apple.

add the leaves

4

Use a dab of glue to affix one leaf to one stem on each apple half.

Designer's Tip: CREATE THE LOOK OF MODULATED SKIN COLOR ON THE EXTERIOR OF THE APPLE BY USING GOLD, ORANGE, AND BURGUNDY COLORED BEADS NEAR THE CORE AND STEM SECTIONS INSTEAD OF RED ONLY.

*Snowbird

*t*ransform a plastic bird into your holiday messenger using feathers and a paper banner you inscribe with your personal sentiments. The feathers are applied to the bird in low graduated layers using glue, while the tail is decorated with a pouf of longer feathers.

materials

plastic or foam bird ✳ acrylic sealer ✳ white acrylic paint
1 bag of white feathers ✳ 8 long plumes, each 6 to 8" long
2 black seed beads ✳ gold micro-glitter
Finished size: 9" from head to tail

you will also need

scissors ✳ X-Acto knife ✳ "T" pin ✳ recycled box lid
foam block ✳ high-tack white glue ✳ 5½" length of
14-gauge steel wire; paint brush ✳ strip of white paper 5"
long by ½" wide ✳ fine-line marker in gold, or as desired

directions

prepare the bird

1

Strip the bird of any decoration, including old feathers
or other covering. Use the knife to cut a ½" wide slice
in the tail area (tail feathers will be inserted here) and a
slice in the beak (banner will be inserted here). Use a
"T" pin to make a pilot hole through the plastic under
the bird's belly in the foot area. Insert the 5½" steel wire
into the hole, pushing it until it meets resistance. Use a
brush to apply sealer to the entire surface of bird; let it
dry thoroughly. Apply an even coat of white paint to all
surfaces; let the paint dry.

2 prepare the feathers

Reserve six 2½" to 3" long feathers. Use a scissors to cut off the top 1¼" section of each feather; save the cut top sections in a box lid and store the stumps for another project. **Note:** Because the bird is small, the feathers must be trimmed down to petal-shaped sections for a more realistic look.

3 glue on the feathers

Stand the bird upright by inserting its wire into the foam block; to form the tail, use the eight long plume feathers only, dipping the quill ends of the feathers into dabs of glue and inserting them into the tail-area slit in a fan shape. To decorate the rest of the bird, use a brush to apply glue to the area adjacent to the tail section. Position and tap down the quill ends of feathers in a ring around the tail, allowing the plumes to overlap one another and the tail feathers. Repeat the process, applying glue to adjacent sections of the bird, and laying down tiers of feathers. Work all the way up to the head, adding a few longer plumes to the crown of the head for drama. Fill in any bare spots with single feathers dipped in glue; use the six reserved untrimmed feathers to form the wings, inserting them into the slits.

4 glitter the beak

Use the brush to apply glue to the beak; then, sprinkle on glitter.

affix the banner

5

Inscribe a personal holiday message on the paper banner; then, slip the paper in the slice in the beak, using a dab of glue to secure it.

optional: snowbird nest in silver wire

materials

20 strands silver bouillon ✴ **optional:** wooden egg painted light turquoise ✴ hot-glue gun and glue stick

directions

1. Hold one strand of bouillon and pull it taut to uncoil the wire.
2. Wrap the strand around your thumb and middle finger to form a round wreath.
3. Stretch a second strand of bouillon and wrap it around the wreath.
4. Repeat the process with the remaining bouillon until a 3" diameter wreath has formed.
5. Hold the wreath and use your thumbs to hollow out a center cavity.
6. Hot-glue a miniature egg painted turquoise in the bottom of the nest.

Designer's Tip: Use feathers in jewel tones or in tropical colors to create birds with a more contemporary style.

Beaded Bugs

*t*hese glass bugs in hard candy colors will glow when they are suspended above the lights on your tree. Made from a row of beads in a variety of unique shapes and sizes, each bug takes only a few minutes to make. First, you string the head and body segments; then you add the wings.

materials

9 glass beads: 1 clear glass, 2 mm; 1 iridescent green, 6 mm
1 red, 12 mm; 1 matte green with polka dots, 14 mm
1 teardrop-shaped emerald green, 6 mm wide by 22 mm
long ✴ 2 leaf-shaped in light green, each 12 mm
wide by 20 mm long ✴ 3 aqua, each 2 mm
28-gauge brass spool wire

you will also need

soft cloth ✴ scissors

directions

arrange the beads

1 Lay the cloth on a flat work surface; arrange the beads in the order listed in the materials list, or in any order that simulates the segments of bug's head, body, and wings.

make the head and body

2 Cut a 9" length of wire; thread the end of the wire into the clear glass bead. Slide the bead to the midpoint of the wire. Fold over the wire, twisting the wires twice at the bead to secure. To string the head and body, thread the wires through one iridescent green, one red, one matte green, one emerald green, and one aqua bead; to secure the beads, bring the ends of the wires around the aqua bead and reinsert them through the emerald green bead, exiting the clear glass bead. Separate the wires into two strands and cut each to a 1¾" length to form the antennae.

make the wings

Cut a 7" length of wire. Thread the end of the wire into one aqua bead. Slide the bead to the midpoint and fold over the wire, twisting the wires twice at the bead to secure. To string the wings, thread the wires into two leaf-shaped beads, round ends facing out. Leave ⅛" length of wire between the beads, using your fingernail to indent the space. Thread the wires through the remaining aqua bead. Bring the ends of the wires around the aqua bead and reinsert them into the leaf bead, exiting the aqua bead. Cut off any excess wire.

attach the wings

Lay the wings perpendicular to the body, pushing the marked center wire between the red and the matte green beads. Bring the wings around to the back of the body, twist them once, and then bring them around to the front, angling them in a flight pattern, or place as desired.

Designer's Tip: RAID YOUR COSTUME JEWELRY BOX, CHOOSING PEARLS OF DIFFERENT TEXTURES TO MAKE ONE LARGE BUG, OR MAKE SEVERAL TINY BUGS, USING FACETED CRYSTAL BEADS IN PASTEL COLORS.

Glitter Balls

*t*his season, instead of using the traditional red and green, why not spell out your holiday message in a field of soft pastel colors like candy pink, mint green, and baby blue? Using self-adhesive letters and numbers, and some micro-glitter, you can greet your guests and family with sentiments like "joy" and "ho-ho-ho," or simply accent the balls with a monogram or the year of the new baby's first Christmas.

materials

glass ball ornament with 2½" to 3" diameter
adhesive lowercase letters, ¾" to 1" high
micro-glitter in soft pastel color, or as desired
Finished size: 2½" diameter

you will also need

glass cleaner ✶ paper towels ✶ plastic straw
masking tape ✶ tweezers ✶ teaspoon ✶ white glue
watercolor paintbrush ✶ X-Acto knife
sheet of plain paper ✶ drinking glass

directions

prepare the ornament

1

Carefully remove the top cap from the ball by pinching the wire loop together with your fingers; ease the wire prongs out of the neck of the ball and set the cap aside. Clean the ball with glass cleaner and paper towels. To secure the "handle," insert the straw into the neck opening and tape around the straw and the neck of the ball.

apply the letters

2

Use tweezers to peel off single letters *j, o* and *y* from the paper backing. Press the letters down in a row around the circumference of the ball. Smooth the edges of each letter with the bowl side of a spoon until they are well adhered.

apply the glitter

3

Hold the ball "handle" and use a paintbrush to coat the surface of the ball with a ⅛" layer of glue, coming up to the edges of the letters but not over them. Hold the ball over a sheet of paper and sprinkle it with glitter, rotating the ball until its entire surface is covered. Stand the ornament upright in a drinking glass by its straw and allow the glue to dry overnight; funnel the glitter back into the container.

remove the letters

4

Use the tip of the knife to carefully lift up the edge of a letter, then slowly peel it off. Repeat the process for all letters; if a letter begins to remove the adjacent glitter coating, lay the letter back down and use the knife to cut along the edge of the letter. Peel and lift off the letter.

replace the cap

5

Replace the cap, being careful to squeeze the wire prongs together to ease them into the ball without breaking the neck.

Designer's Tip: AFTER LETTERS ARE POSITIONED, APPLY NARROW STRIPS OF TAPE IN HORIZONTAL BANDS, THEN GLUE AND GLITTER EACH SECTION A DIFFERENT COLOR TO CREATE STRIPES.

Open Hoops with Bow

*t*he sparkling hoops of this open ball ornament are made simply by wrapping wire around an ordinary soup can. When the hoops are wired together, they form an open ball. The hoops are decorated with strands of green beads, then accented with a light dusting of matching glitter.

materials

soup can with 3" diameter ✴ 18-gauge galvanized
steel wire ✴ 28-gauge brass spool wire
beads: 3 strands in clear chartreuse, each 2mm
1 strand clear crystal with metallic silver linings, 2mm
micro-glitter in chartreuse

you will also need

ruler ✴ wire cutters ✴ round-nose pliers
narrow paintbrush ✴ high-tack glue

directions

make the hoops

1

Measure and cut two 10½" lengths of galvanized wire,
using a ruler and wire cutters. To form one hoop, hold
the end of one length of wire against the soup can and
wrap it around the can, overlapping the wire ends; slip
the hoop off the can and bind the overlap, using 28-
gauge wire; repeat the process to make the second hoop.

2 string the beads

Cut three 25" lengths of 28-gauge wire. Set two aside. On wire, twist and crimp one end to secure the beads. Insert the opposite end of the wire into enough green seed beads to make a 23" strand. Twist and crimp the end of the wire, but do not cut off extra wire, as this will provide easements.

3 decorate the hoops

Hold the end of a strand of chartreuse beads against the top surface of one hoop at the overlap. Wrap the end of a separate 25" length of fine wire two times around the beginning of the strand and the hoop, laying the wire between the beads. Lash the strand of beads to the hoop until it reaches the beginning (do not cut the strand of beads) slip the bare second hoop inside the decorated hoop, with the overlapped sections touching. If a bead interferes, adjust the beads to make way for the intersection. Bind the intersections at the overlap and at the opposite pole using short lengths of 28-gauge wire. Decorate the second hoop by turning the strand of beads 90 degrees, using the remaining 25" length of wire to lash the strand of beads to the hoop until it meets the overlap at the top. To end off, wrap available fine wire around the end of the strand of beads, trimming off the extra beads, if necessary; then, clip the wires and crimp the ends.

accent the hoops with glitter

4

Use a paint brush to apply a thin coat of glue to all exposed wire and sprinkle it with glitter. Let the glue dry.

make the beaded bow

5

Measure and cut a 14" length of fine spool wire. Twist and crimp one end to secure the beads; then, string on crystal seed beads, leaving ½" free at the end. Reinsert the end of the wire into the last bead and pull taut to secure the strand. Shape a two-loop bow, twisting the loops at the center to secure them. Use short length of fine wire to affix the bow to the top of the hoops at the overlap.

Designer's Tip: SUSPEND A SMALL BALL ORNAMENT WITHIN THE INTERSECTING BALLS, USING A LENGTH OF WIRE TO AFFIX THE CAP OF THE ORNAMENT UNDER THE HOOPS.

French Café Chair

*C*reate a souvenir ornament of one of the most romantic cities in the world—Paris. This metal chair is inspired by those chairs found at sidewalk cafés along the banks of the Seine River. You can fashion one using twisted wire, the lid from a tin, and a scrap of velvet.

materials

18-gauge armature wire ✳ lid from 1⅜" diameter tin

you will also need

ruler ✳ wire cutters ✳ round-nose pliers
28-gauge spool wire ✳ marker ✳ five-minute epoxy glue
plastic lid ✳ toothpicks ✳ hot-glue gun ✳ glue sticks
sewing needle ✳ red thread

directions

form the chair back

1

See the chair back diagram on page 114. Measure and cut three 15" lengths from armature wire. Fold each length in half. Tightly twist the wires together to form rods, using the pliers to secure a good grip at the fold. Measure and cut each rod to 7". Use pliers to form a coil on the fold end of a rod. Repeat the process on a second rod. Set the rods aside. To form the center detail, fold the remaining rod in half, crossing one wire over the other; form a C-shaped coil at the end of each wire, using pliers. Lay the coiled rods on a flat surface with coils facing each other. Insert the fold section of the third rod in between the coils. Bind them at contact point, indicated by a red dot on the diagram, using spool wire.

75

form the legs

2 Measure and cut four 6½" lengths of armature wire. Make one leg by folding one wire in half and tightly twisting the wires together to form a stiff rod; allow a small loop form at the fold. Use the pliers to bend up the loop to form a foot. Repeat the process to make three more legs with feet. Measure and cut each leg to 2¾" long, using a ruler and wire cutters. Set the legs aside.

make the seat hoop

3 Measure and cut a 10" length of armature wire. Fold the wire in half and tightly twist it into a stiff rod. Use your hands and pliers to shape a hoop that is slightly smaller than diameter of lid. Cut off excess wire. Turn lid wrong side up, and fit the hoop inside.

attach the legs to the hoop

4 Untwist one twist in the end of each wire leg. Using a marker and the clock as orientation, mark four leg positions on the hoop at 12, 3, 6, and 9. Straddle one leg on one mark of the hoop. Squeeze the leg wires to the hoop. Repeat the process for the remaining legs. Following the manufacturer's directions, mix up a small batch of five-minute epoxy glue in a plastic lid. Use a toothpick to apply blobs of glue to each leg at the hoop position and around the inside of the hoop.

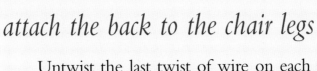

attach the back to the chair legs 5

Untwist the last twist of wire on each side of the chair back. Use pliers to bend the wires around the back of each chair leg. Using a dab of five-minute epoxy, reinforce the join. Curve the wires around the back of the lid, if necessary, to accommodate the lid rim. Adjust the legs of the chair and the chair back so that it stands upright.

make the cushion 6

See pattern on page 114. Measure and cut a 2" diameter circle from the velvet scrap, using the pattern. Use a hand-sewing needle and thread to sew a basting stitch around the edge of the circle, ⅛" from the edge. Gather the velvet along the thread to create a pouch. Flatten the pouch to form a disk. Test-fit the velvet disk so that it lies within the perimeter of the chair seat. Adjust the gathers, as necessary. Secure the gathers with a few tiny stitches. Using tiny dabs of hot-glue, glue the cushion to the chair seat.

Designer's Tip: SPRAY-PAINT THE CHAIR GOLD, THEN ADD A VELVET CUSHION MADE IN COBALT BLUE; OR DECORATE THE SEAT WITH RHINESTONES.

Potted Topiaries

a little forest of pine trees stands in English-style planters complete with ball feet and beaded finials. The secret behind these conifers are bristle brushes made for baby bottles. All you do is snip away at the bristles until you have shaped them into slender or broad cones.

materials

bristle brush ✳ spray paint: green and whitewash
mat board ✳ acrylic paint in light yellow
gold paint marker ✳ beads: 4 gold, each 12 mm;
8 pearl, each 4mm; 8 green glass, each 2 mm
Finished size: 5" high by 1½" wide

you will also need

spray adhesive ✳ scissors ✳ wire cutters ✳ pencil
X-Acto knife ✳ straight-edge ruler ✳ hot-glue gun
glue sticks ✳ watercolor paintbrush ✳ foam core

directions

Note: The size of the tree will be determined by the width of the brush. Adjust the size of the pot to the width measurement. The potted topiary is proportioned so that the tree is ⅔ and the pot is ⅓ of the total measurement.

prepare the brush

Use wire cutters to cut off the hanging loop from the end of the handle; discard the loop.

1

shape the cone

Use scissors to cut the brush into a cone shape, turning the brush around to view it from all sides. Trim the bristles until the tree measures 2¾" tall and 1¾" wide at its base, or cut to any other desired size.

2

paint the tree

3 Spray-paint the tree green; let the paint dry. Apply a light coat of whitewash to quiet down the green color.

copy and affix the pot patterns to the board

4 Photocopy the pattern for the pot and the corner strip on page 121. Use an X-Acto knife and a ruler to cut out the patterns. Spray a light coat of adhesive to the wrong side of the patterns; then press the pattern pieces on the board.

cut out the pot

5 Use a straight-edge ruler and an X-Acto knife to cut out the pot template along the marked lines: Score the dash lines using light pressure on the knife without cutting through the board, and cut all the way through the board along the bold lines by applying firmer pressure on the knife. Remove the pattern from the mat board; cut out the corner strip, as before.

fold and glue the pot sections

6 Fold the pot on the score lines so that the scoring faces out. Hot-glue the free edge to the edge of the adjacent wall to form a box using a corner strip to reinforce the join. Apply a line of glue to the edges of the box bottom, then bring it up to meet the walls of the box and glue it in place. Let the glue dry.

paint the pot

7

Use a brush to apply a coat of yellow paint to all surfaces of the box, including the inside rim. Let the paint dry. Draw parallel stripes on each side of the box, using a paint marker and a ruler; let the paint dry.

"plant" the tree

8

Use wire cutters to cut the tree stem so the tree measures 4" from top to bottom. (**Note:** The bare section of the wire stem will measure about 1¾" long). Mark and cut a 1⅜" square from the foam core. Using the wire stem of the tree, bore a hole in the center of the foam. Slide the foam up to the bottom rim of the "branches." Apply a liberal blob of glue to the interior floor of the box, then immediately insert the stem of the tree into the glue. Hold the tree straight until the glue hardens (about 1 minute). Apply a line of white glue to the edges of the foam core, then slide the foam down, fitting it inside the box ⅛" below the box rim.

decorate the pot

9

Turn the potted tree over. Use hot-glue to attach one gold bead to each corner of the pot. Turn the potted tree right side up. For each finial, insert a straight pin into two green beads and two pearls. Push the pin into the corner of the pot. Use hot-glue to affix the star to the top of the tree.

Designer's Tip: USE MINIATURE TERRA COTTA POTS FOR THE TREES INSTEAD OF MAKING THE POTS FROM MAT BOARD.

Little Village Houses

Create your own little village right on the branches of your Christ-mas tree by nestling these charming cottages in clusters among the other ornaments. The added charm of these cottages is their glowing windows, created by inserting a bulb from the minilights into the small hole cut into the base of each house.

materials

1 sheet white mat board ✳ 1 8½" by 11" sheet of vellum
acrylic paint: red, yellow, white, black, and green
balsa wood stick, ⅜" square
Yield: 4 houses
Finished size: 2¼" wide x 2½" high

you will also need

pencil ✳ X-Acto knife ✳ straight-edge ruler
spray adhesive ✳ paintbrushes: watercolor and fine line
white glue ✳ hot-glue gun ✳ glue sticks
fake snow in fine grain

directions

copy and affix the patterns to the board

1

Photocopy four pattern pieces for each of the four houses on page 119. On a protected work surface, use an X-Acto knife and ruler to cut out the patterns. Working in a well-ventilated room, spray a light coat of adhesive to the wrong side of each pattern piece; then, press the pattern pieces on the board.

2 cut out the house sections

Use an X-Acto knife and a straight-edge ruler to cut out all the sections for the four houses: Score the dash lines by using light pressure on the knife without cutting through the board. Cut all the way through the board along the bold lines by applying firmer pressure to the knife. Cut out the windows, saving the cutouts to use as shutters.

3 add the windows and doors

Mark and cut four doors from scrap board, each ⅝" by 1⅛" and sixteen squares of vellum, each 1¼" square. Turn the house wall sections face down. Glue one vellum square over each window opening. Glue one door over each door cutout for the look of a recessed opening.

4 fold and glue the house sections

Fold the houses on the score lines so that the scoring faces out. Hot-glue the free edge to the edge of the adjacent wall to form a box, using corner strip to reinforce join. Bore a ⅜" diameter hole in the center of each base, using a scissor blade. Use your finger to tamp down the ragged paper edge with white glue. Position each house on its base. Apply a liberal line of glue along the interior side of the bottom of the walls and the base. Repeat the process for all houses. Fold the roof sections on the score lines so that the scoring faces out. Position and hot-glue the roofs to the houses. Add the shutters if desired. Optional chimney: Use the X-Acto knife to cut an angle on one side of the ¾" length of balsa wood. To affix chimney, position on one side of roof, using hot glue to secure.

paint the houses

5 Use the watercolor brush to apply white paint to each base, yellow paint to all the walls, red paint to each roof, and black to each chimney; use a fine-line paintbrush to apply green paint to the doors and shutters.

apply the snow

6 Work in a well-ventilated room. Set the houses on a protected work surface. Pour a cup of fake snow in a bowl. Apply a sweeping spray of adhesive over the houses, then immediately sprinkle a liberal handful of snow over the glued areas, throwing snow at the sides of the house to simulate a snow storm.

Designer's Tip: ADD INTERESTING ARCHITECTURAL DETAIL TO THE HOUSES: AFFIX FILIGREE BEADS ALONG THE PEAK OF THE ROOF; BRUSH ON LINES OF FABRIC PAINT TO SIMULATE SIMPLE MULLION WINDOWS; STACK STRIPS OF BALSA WOOD FOR STEPS; AND GLUE BRASS CHARMS IN CURLICUE SHAPES TO SUGGEST STONE CARVINGS OVER THE DOORWAY.

Glitter Fish with Lures

*t*hese whimsical fish are decorated in shimmering colors using very fine glitter. The jazzy patterns are made possible by applying the glue in realistic patterns using a paintbrush, then sprinkling the glue with glitter.

materials

2 flexible plastic fish, each 3¾" long ✳ micro-glitter:
[for both fish]: royal blue; [blue fish]: baby blue and
highlight warm; [green fish]: emerald green,
lime green, and pink ✳ 4 royal blue or
white diamond rhinestones, each 4mm
Finished size: 3¾" long

you will also need

2 J-hook posts for pierced earrings
watercolor paintbrush ✳ high-tack glue
6 sheets of white paper

directions

prepare the fish

1

Insert the end of one J-shaped post into the mouth section of one fish; repeat the process for the second fish.
Note: These hooks will act as handles and as decoration.

decorate the body

2

On both fish, one at a time, use a paintbrush to apply a
light coat of glue to both sides of the fins and the tails.
Work over a sheet of paper and sprinkle on royal blue
glitter; gently tap off the excess.

3 on the blue fish

Repeat the process on both sides of the fish to apply royal blue glitter to the top third, baby blue glitter to the midsection, and highlight warm glitter to the lower third of the body. Let the glue dry about five minutes. To add detail, use a paintbrush to apply a thin, wavy line of glue between the midsection and the lower third of the fish on both sides. Sprinkle with royal blue glitter. Funnel each color of glitter back into its container.

4 on the green fish

Repeat the process on both sides of the fish to apply emerald green glitter to the top third, lime green glitter to the midsection, and pink glitter to the bottom third of the body. Let the glue dry about five minutes. To add details, use a paintbrush to apply dots of glue on the midsection. Sprinkle with royal blue glitter. Funnel each color of glitter back into its container.

5 glue on the eyes

Use the paintbrush to apply a dot of glue to each eye, then press on one rhinestone. Allow the glue to dry.

Designer's Tip: MAKE UP YOUR OWN PATTERNS, LIKE POLKA DOTS AND ZEBRA STRIPES, ON THE SIDE OF EACH FISH, IF YOU PREFER.

optional: lures

materials

2 j-hook posts for pierced earrings ✳ 2 beads, each 4mm
2 small brass charms with hanging loops, as desired
2½" long white feathers ✳ 2 1" long sections
of satin ribbon in light blue, ⅛" wide

you will also need

round-nose pliers ✳ brown cotton thread ✳ hightack glue

directions

prepare the hook

1

Use the pliers to straighten out the curve on the j-hook.
Insert the end of the wire into one bead and one charm;
then use the pliers to rebend the hook into a j-shape.

make the lures

2

Fold one ribbon section in half; hold the tip of one quill
(not the feather) against the fold in the ribbon and press
them against the top section of the hook finding. Bind
the section together with thread. Smear a dab of glue to
reinforce the secure join. Repeat the process to make
the second lure.

Silver Snowflakes

*t*he simple elegance of these snowflakes is that each is made using the same method, yet each design is distinctly different and beautiful. Although nature may precipitate only six-pointed snowflakes, you can make snowflakes with more spokes and in a variety of different sizes, if you like. All you do is twist pipe cleaners together and add short lengths to the spokes to simulate the frosty details found in nature.

materials

12 metallic silver pipe cleaners
Finished size: 6½" diameter

you will also need

ruler ✻ junky scissors

directions

1 *prepare the pipe cleaners*

For the base of the six-point snowflake, measure and cut six 6½" long pipe cleaners, using a ruler and scissors; arrange the pipe cleaners in pairs of two; for the arm details, measure and cut twelve 2¼" lengths from the remaining pipe cleaners.

2 *make a six-spoke snowflake*

Refer to the diagram on page 122. Twist two 6½" long pipe cleaners together. Twist a 3" section of the next pair. Trap the twisted pair between the wires at its mid-point, forming an X, and continue to twist the remaining length of the wires together. Repeat the process to attach the remaining pair of pipe cleaners, bisecting the X already formed. Adjust the spokes so that the space between them is equal.

add the frosty details

Decorate one spoke at a time, positioning the midpoint of one short length over one spoke of the snowflake in whatever position is indicated by the red dot, or as desired. Fold the ends behind the spoke, twist them once, and bring the ends back to the front on an even plane with the spoke. Repeat the process to affix two frosty details to each spoke of the snowflake, or as desired. **Optional:** Trim the ends of each detail to simulate the variety in nature.

✳

Designer's Tip: Color your snowflakes sparkling colors. Make the snowflake, spray it with adhesive, then sprinkle on any color glitter you please; tap off the excess, saving the glitter in the vial.

Jeweled Pears

*t*he elegance of these miniature pears is made possible by varying the size, texture, and shimmer of the applied decoration. With just a handful of beads, pearls and rhinestones, all in tones of white and silver, and a smattering of some paint and glue, you can transform ordinary plastic pears into jeweled accents for the tree.

materials

3 foam pears with leaves, 1¾" to 2½" high
beads: 36 strands, each 20" ✶ clear seed beads
pearls in assorted sizes, 2mm to 4mm
24 diamond rhinestones, 4mm to 5mm
white acrylic paint

you will also need

aluminum wire ✶ wire cutters ✶ pliers
sponge brush, 1" wide ✶ high-tack glue
five-minute epoxy glue ✶ toothpicks ✶ recycled lids
from shoebox and yogurt containers ✶ teaspoon

directions

1

prepare the fruit

For hanging hooks, cut three 3½" lengths of aluminum wire using wire cutters. Bend one end of each length into a tiny hook, using pliers. Push the opposite end of the wire into the bottom of the pear, exiting out the top stem area. Bend the top wires into hooks. Paint the pears white, including the leaves, using the sponge brush. Let the paint dry.

2

prepare the beads

Set the empty shoebox lid on a flat work surface. Cut the threads on the strands of seed beads, allowing the beads to collect in the lid. Empty each package of the other decorations—beads, pearls, and rhinestones—into a separate container lid.

apply the seed beads

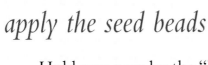

Hold one pear by the "handle" and squeeze white glue directly on one quarter of fruit's surface; smooth the glue into an even coat, using the sponge brush. Hold the pear over the box lid and use a teaspoon to sprinkle the seed beads over the glued surface. Lay the fruit in one corner of the box lid. Repeat the gluing and beading process with the remaining pears, then, continue as before, decorating small adjacent sections of each piece of fruit until all surfaces of the pears are covered with beads. Let the glue dry.

apply the pearls and the rhinestones

Work in a well-ventilated room. Mix up a small batch of 5-minute epoxy following the manufacturer's directions. Use the tweezers to pick up and hold a single pearl or rhinestone; dip one side of the jewel into the epoxy glue. Immediately position the single jewel in either a bare space on the pear or in a second layer over the layer of seed beads. Repeat the process to accent the pear with more pearls and rhinestones in positions as desired.

Designer's Tip: SUBSTITUTE THE BEADS AND RHINESTONES WITH MICRO-GLITTER, APPLYING THE GLITTER IN ICY BLUE, BABY BLUE, LIGHT BLUE, AND DIAMOND TO ADJACENT SECTIONS TO ACHIEVE MODULATED COLOR.

Glitter Butterflies

*Y*ou can almost hear the fluttering sound of these butterflies, they are so light and sparkling. Easy to cut out of foil, each butterfly is lathered with glue and sprinkled with very fine glitter in pastel shades.

materials

36-gauge aluminum tooling foil * micro-glitter in pastel
shades: baby blue, baby pink, fuschia, lime green
Finished size: 3" wide by 3½" high

you will also need

scissors: straight blade and manicure * soft cloth
denatured alcohol * cotton balls * masking tape
X-Acto knife * stylus * watercolor paintbrush
white glue * 5 sheets of paper * "T" pin
wooden skewer * ruler * acrylic spray sealer in gloss
28-gauge brass spool wire

directions

prepare the patterns

1

Photocopy the pattern on page 115 five times to make
five butterflies. Neatly cut out the patterns along the
heavy line.

cut out the foil butterflies

2

Work in a well-ventilated room on a protected work
surface. Unroll a 12" length of foil, smoothing it flat with
a soft cloth. Clean the surface of the foil with denatured
alcohol and a cotton ball. Tape the patterns, right side up,
to the foil. Rough-cut the butterflies from the foil, using
an X-Acto knife. Use the manicure scissors to make
more precise cuts around the pattern outlines all around.

3 draw the wing pattern

Lay the butterflies on a flat work surface. Working with one at a time, use a stylus to trace the dash lines of the wing patterns and eye positions, pressing hard enough to indent the foil. Remove the paper patterns.

4 apply the glitter

Lay each butterfly on a separate sheet of paper. Begin with one butterfly, using a paintbrush to apply glue to corresponding sections on both wings. Sprinkle on the chosen color glitter directly from the container, catching the excess on the paper. Let the butterfly rest. Meanwhile, repeat the process, gluing and glittering corresponding wing sections on the remaining butterflies. Let the glue dry. Go back to the first butterfly, shake off first color glitter, then apply glue to the second wing sections. Repeat the process, applying glitter and allowing the glue to dry. Turn the butterflies over and repeat the process to glue and glitter the backs of the wings.

attach the antennae

5

Use the "T" pin to make two holes at the marked positions in the head of one butterfly. Measure and cut two 4" lengths of wire. Thread one wire halfway through each hole, then fold and twist the wires together to secure. Repeat the process for the other antenna.

hang the butterflies

6

Use the "T" pin to make a hole in the center of the body. Thread a 5" length of wire through the hole, twisting a loop underneath the body to secure. Repeat the process for the remaining butterflies. Lay the wooden skewer along the body section and push the foil around the skewer. Slide out the skewer and suspend the butterfly by the wire.

Designer's Tip: CREATE YOUR OWN WING PATTERNS, USING THE STYLUS, THEN COLOR THEM IN DIFFERENT SHADES OF ONE COLOR. OR, APPLY A SMALL DAB OF GLUE OVER AN ALREADY GLITTERED WING, SPRINKLE WITH CONTRASTING GLITTER, AND YOU CAN ADD SNAZZY POLKA DOTS!

Miniature Chandeliers

*N*ow glacial-looking chandeliers can hang from the boughs of your Christmas tree. All you need is some plain wire and glass beads. The chandelier can be plain, with only four arms ending in candles, or it can be more elaborate, having a beaded stem accented with wire curlicues and crystal teardrops.

materials

For the crystal chandelier:
18-gauge galvanized steel wire ✳ 28-gauge aluminum wire
For decoration:
crystals: round: 6, each 10 mm; 1, 16 mm
teardrop: 16, each 14 mm
Finished size: 4" high by 4" wide

you will also need

wire cutters ✳ round-nose pliers ✳ five-minute epoxy
wooden toothpicks ✳ plastic lid ✳ correction fluid
hot-glue gun ✳ glue stick

directions

prepare the wire

1

Refer to the diagram on page 115. From the 18-gauge steel wire, measure and cut a 5" length for the central stem, four 5½" lengths for the arms, four 6" lengths for the large S-shaped curlicues, and four 4" lengths for the small C-shaped curlicues, using wire cutters

form the central stem

2

Use pliers to form a small hook on one end of the 5" length of wire. Insert the opposite end into seven crystal beads in the following order: 10mm, 16mm, and five 10mm. End off the wire by crimping it to keep the beads from sliding off. Set the stem aside.

103

3 form the J-shaped arms

Use pliers to form a small hook on one end of the 5½" length of wire; bend the wire ½" from the hook, then shape a J beginning the curve of the J 2¼" from the bend. Make the candle holder at the end of the wire by using pliers to twist the wire two to three times to make a coil shape. Set the arm aside. Repeat the process to make three more arms.

4 make the curlicues

Use pliers to twist the end of one 6" length two to three times to form a flat coil. Repeat the process at the other end of the wire. Make the remaining three curlicues following the same process. Form an S-shaped curlicue by holding curls in opposite hands and twisting one curl. To make the small C-shaped curlicues, follow the same process as before, but omit the twist action.

5 decorate the arms

Following the diagram on page 115, position and affix one C-shaped and one S-shaped curlicue, using fine wire.

Designer's Tip: IF YOU WANT TO SPLURGE, BUY SILVER WIRE TO MAKE YOUR CHANDELIER AND STRING CUT CRYSTALS INTO LONG STRANDS, DRAPING THEM BETWEEN THE ARMS OF THE CHANDELIER.

assemble the chandelier

Using pliers, uncrimp the top end of the central stem. Insert the end of the wire into the hook at the end of one J-shaped arm, allowing the hook to slide down to the top of the first bead. Slip on the remaining three arms, allowing them to rest on one another. Lay the chandelier on a flat surface. Follow the manufacturer's directions to mix up a small batch of five-minute epoxy glue in plastic lid using a toothpick. Hold the chandelier by the stem at the top and dab epoxy glue on the hooks of each arm to secure them to the stem. Arrange the arms evenly around the central stem. Let the glue dry. Secure the midsection of each arm to the central stem using a short length of fine wire, adding a round bead to span the gap, if necessary. Trim the excess wire at the top of the central stem, using pliers to form a small hook for a hanger.

make and install the candles

Use scissors to trim four toothpicks to 1¼"; paint the sections, with correction fluid. Let the fluid dry. Insert one candle into each coil candle cup, securing each with a dab of epoxy. For the candle flames, use a dab of hot glue, pulling up the nozzle of the gun to form a point. For candle drips, apply correction fluid to the sides of the candles as desired.

add the hanging crystals

Wire the teardrop crystals with 1" lengths of fine wire. Affix the crystals to positions on the arms as desired, twisting the wire to secure.

Velvet Cornucopia

*h*ere is a modern take on the cornucopia, one of the most traditional decorations of all. Made from lush velvet, the cone
shape is sleek in line and rich in texture. To add a retro-style,
accent the ornament with an oversized daisy in cherry red.

materials

12" square of red rayon velvet ✳ 12" square
giftwrap paper ✳ lightweight Bristol board
Finished size: 5½" high; 4" diameter top opening

you will also need

craft paper ✳ tracing paper ✳ pencil ✳ compass
X-Acto knife ✳ straight-edge ruler ✳ scissors
stiff brush ✳ transparent stick-flat glue ✳ waxed paper
heavy book ✳ 2 craft sticks ✳ 1 spring-clip clothes pin
optional: artificial flower with 4" diameter
hot-glue gun ✳ glue stick

directions

trace and cut out the template

1

Photocopy the pattern on page 117, then rough-cut ½"
beyond the marked lines all around. Tape the pattern
right side up to the Bristol board. Using an X-Acto
knife and straight-edged ruler to cut the straight sides;
and a scissor to cut along the marked curve, cut out a
cornucopia template along solid line from the Bristol
board.

cut out the lining

2

Use the template to mark and cut out a lining from
giftwrap paper.

3 cut out the velvet

Lay the velvet right side down on a protected work surface. Lay the template on the craft paper. Brush the template with glue, including edges. Lay the template, glue side down, on the velvet, allowing at least 1" all around. Smooth the velvet flat and let the glue dry. Trim the excess velvet to ½" from all the edges. Clip across the corners. On the shorter straight edge, trim the velvet even with the board, then notch the velvet around the arc.

4 glue the velvet to the template

Brush glue onto the wrong side of the velvet allowances notched around the arc of the template. Fold and press down the velvet onto the board. Repeat the process to glue and fold the allowance at the longer straight edge. Lay the cornucopia wrong side down on waxed paper and weight it with a book. Let the glue dry.

5 shape the cornucopia

Cut the sticks 1" shorter than the height of the template. Roll the template into a cone so that the longer straight edge overlaps the trimmed edge as indicated on the pattern. Roll it tightly so that the cone holds its shape. Let it unroll. Carefully apply glue to the wrong side of the longer straight edge. Shape the template into a cone until longer straight edge overlaps shorter straight edge and meets dash line. Clip one craft stick to either side of the overlap. Let the glue dry, then remove the sticks.

glue in the ribbon handle

6

Apply a dab of glue to opposite interior sides of the cornucopia near the top edge. Position and press the ends of the ribbon against the glue; let the glue dry.

glue in the lining

7

Roll the lining into a cone and insert it into the cornucopia. Mark any extra paper that extends above the top edge. Remove the lining and trim off the excess. Apply glue to the inside of the cornucopia. Reroll the lining and reinsert it into the cornucopia. Press the lining against the walls. Let the glue dry.

attach the flower

8

Position and glue flower to cornucopia, as shown, using hot-glue.

Designer's Tip: GLUE ON SMALL SILK FLOWERS IN AN OVERALL PATTERN OR JUST AROUND THE RIM OF THE CORNUCOPIA. USE A DAB OF HOT GLUE TO AFFIX EACH BLOOM.

Tree-Top Star

*t*his eight-point double star is a simple but majestic reference to the Star of Bethlehem. Made brilliant with fine glitter in ice blue and silver, the secret of the star's construction is that the smaller star is actually cut out of the center of the larger star and rotated to reveal the spire-shaped cutouts.

materials

2 16" squares of white mat board ✳ 8 gold filigree beads,
each 18 mm ✳ micro-glitter in ice blue and silver

you will also need

sheet of tracing paper ✳ straight-edge ruler ✳ pencil
X-Acto knife ✳ heavy-duty tape ✳ paintbrush ✳ wire cutters
8 extra-long straight pins ✳ 18-gauge steel wire
broom handle ✳ spray adhesive ✳ five-minute epoxy glue
plastic lid ✳ toothpicks ✳ white glue

directions

enlarge the pattern

Enlarge the pattern on page 123 using a copy.

1

cut out the stars

Note: For a clean cut, lightly run the blade of the X-Acto knife along the edge of the ruler to score the line, then repeat the motion with more pressure to cut through the board. Lay the squares of mat board together on a protected work surface, taping their edges to prevent shifting. Lay the copied star pattern over the boards. Use a ruler and an X-acto knife to cut through both boards along all marked lines as follows: Cut out the small central star along the fine line; then repeat the process to cut out the larger star along the heavy line.

2

3

apply the glitter

Separate the cut-out stars, keeping the same-size sections together. Lay the small central stars on scrap paper on a protected work surface, right side up. Use a paintbrush to apply a thick coat of white glue to the top and edges of both stars. Sprinkle the glued areas with a liberal layer of ice blue glitter, collecting and returning the extra glitter to the container. Let the glue dry. Repeat the process to apply the glue and the silver glitter to the right sides and edges of the larger stars.

4

attach the stars

Lay the large stars on the work surface, glitter side up. Lay the blue central stars within the original cutout. **Note:** the smaller star will not fit inside the original cutout; this is for position only. Rotate the smaller star 15 to 20 degrees until the points of the star poke into the center of the cutout. Following the manufacturer's directions, mix up a small batch of five-minute epoxy. Use dabs of the epoxy to secure the position of the smaller star to the larger one. Repeat the process to position and secure the second set of stars.

assemble the stars

5

Measure and cut a 30" length of wire, using a ruler and wire cutters. Fold the wire in half and twist the lengths together; shape a coil base by wrapping the bottom 4" of the wire around a broom handle. **Note:** Tree top is inserted into coil. Then, attach the wire to the stars. Lay the stars wrong side up on a flat work surface. Center the twisted wire along the red dash line on one star, using one long strip of tape to secure the wire. Spray a coat of adhesive on the wrong sides of both stars, then press them together, all edges, even to adhere them, and to trap the wire stem inside. Set the star aside.

attach the beads to the points of large star

6

Insert one pin into each gold bead. Insert the pin between the boards of the stars at each point. Use a dab of epoxy to secure the bead at each point, repeat for remaining beads.

Designer's Tip: MAKE A PATTERN OF THE CENTER STAR, USING A PHOTOCOPY MACHINE TO REDUCE ITS SIZE TO 40 PERCENT. CUT OUT THE PATTERN AND USE IT TO MARK AND CUT OUT A THIRD STAR FROM MAT BOARD. APPLY GLUE FOLLOWED BY GLITTER, THEN LET IT DRY. USE HOT-GLUE TO AFFIX IT TO THE CENTER OF THE SMALL STAR.

Suggested Patterns

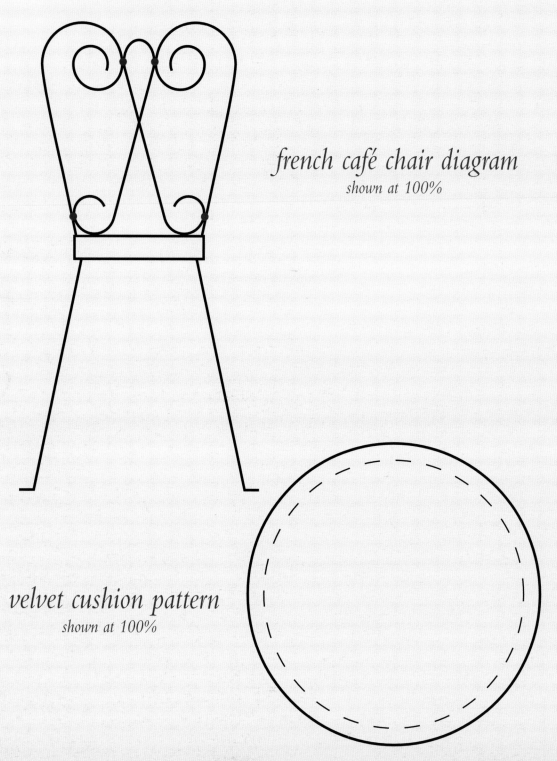

french café chair diagram
shown at 100%

velvet cushion pattern
shown at 100%

miniature chandelier diagram

shown at 100%

glitter butterfly pattern

shown at 100%

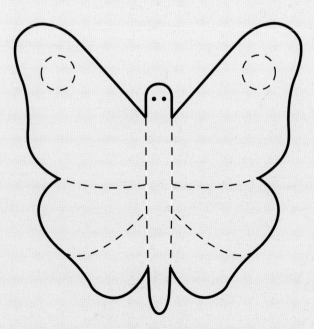

paper pine tree - two tiers
shown at 100%

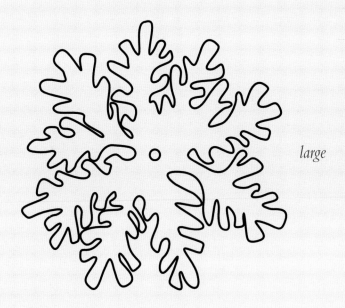

large

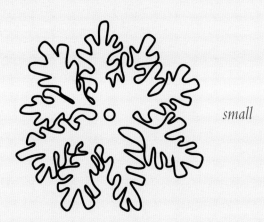

small

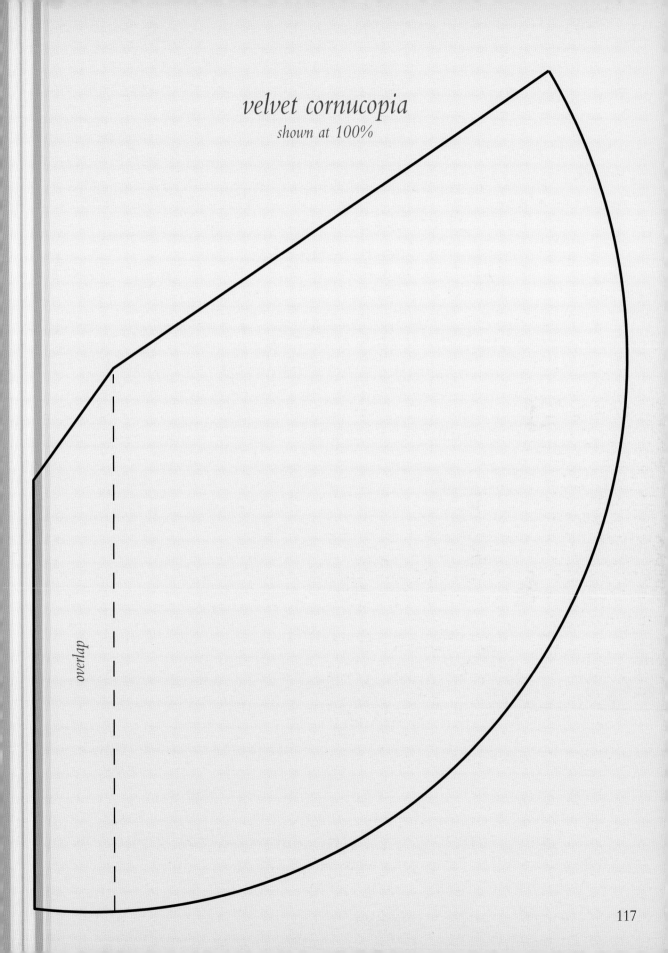

velvet cornucopia
shown at 100%

overlap

velvet slipper
shown at 100%

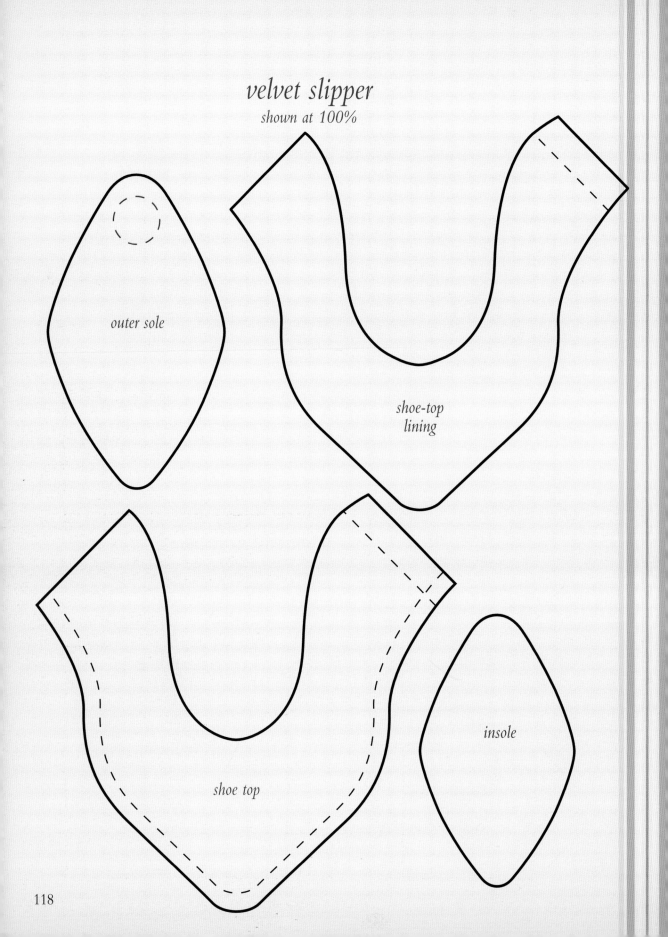

outer sole

shoe-top lining

shoe top

insole

little village house
shown at 100%

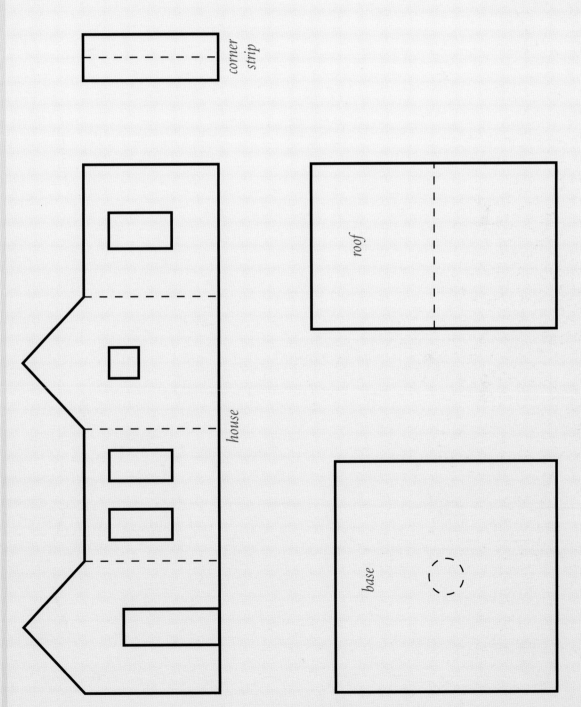

corner
strip

roof

house

base

jeweled snap pea - pod, stem leaves and leaf
shown at 100%

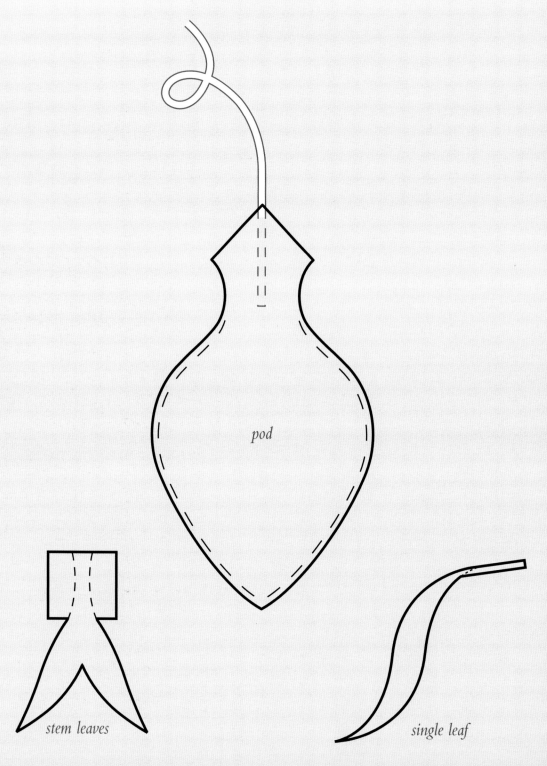

pod

stem leaves

single leaf

potted topiary: pot (container)

shown at 100%

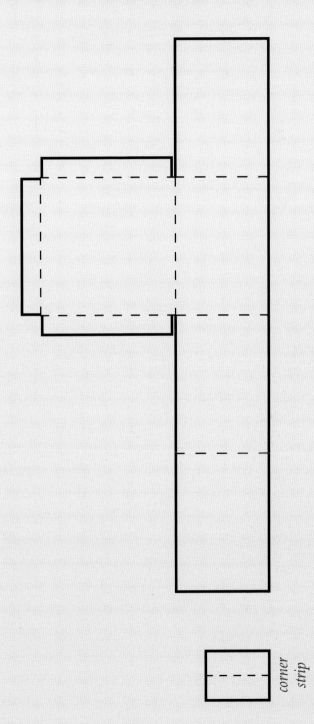

corner
strip

silver snowflake

shown at 100%

tree-top star
shown at 50%

Material List

Ornament:	material	color	form
Striped Balls	Glass/tape	Red	Round
Chandelier Crystal Wreaths	Wire/beads	Clear	Hoop
Jeweled Snap Peas	Foil/rhinstns	Green	Natural
Old-Fashioned Tinsel	Foil/mrkr	Pastels	Stick
Time Capsule Timepieces	Metal/findings	Gold	Round
Ballet Tutus	Ribbon tulle	Pastel	Free
Velvet Slippers	Paper/velvet	Red	Styled
Etched Glass Balls	Glass/etch	Clear	Round
Charm Wreaths	Metal charms	Brass	Hoop
Paper Pine Trees	Skewer/paper	White	Natural
Hinged Scallop Shells	Shells/beads	Gold/white	Natural
Beaded Apple Halves	Foam/beads	Red/white	Natural
Snowbird	Plastic/feathers	White/silver	Natural
Beaded Bugs	Wire/beads	Multi/jewel	Natural
Glitter Balls	Glass/glitter	Mint green	Round
Open Hoops with Bow	Wire/beads	Mint green	Hoops
French Café Chair	Wire/velvet	Silver/red	Styled
Potted Topiaries	Brush/paper	Green/yellow	Cone
Little Village Houses	Paper/paint	Yellow/red	Box
Glitter Fish with Lures	Plastic/glitter	Blue/green	Natural
Silver Snowflakes	Pipe cleaners	Silver	Natural
Jeweled Pears	Beads/rhinstns	White/silver	Natural
Glitter Butterflies	Foil/glitter	Pastel	Natural
Miniature Chandeliers	Wire/crystals	Silver/clear	Styled
Velvet Cornucopia	Paper/velvet	Red	Cone
Tree-Top Star	Paper/glitter	Silver/ice blue	Star

*Sources

*t*he general references below are for sources that sell basic craft materials. For specific craft items that are more difficult to find, consult the alphabetized list of materials and contact the company for more information or for a retail distributor near you.

general

Craft King, Inc.
3033 Drane Field Road,
Suite 5
Lakeland, FL 33811
(800) CRAFTY-1
Fax: (941) 648-2972
Web site: craftkng@gate.net

Dick Blick Art Materials
695 U.S. Highway
East Galesburg, IL 61401
(800) 447-8192
Fax: (800) 621-8293
Web site: www.dickblick.com

Michael's Arts and Crafts
8000 Bent Branch Drive
Irving, TX 75063
(800) MICHAELS
Web site: www.michaels.com

Pearl Paint
308 Canal Street
New York, NY 10013-2572
(800) 451-7327
Fax: (212) 274-8290
Web site: www.pearlpaint.com

Sunshine Discount Crafts
12335 62nd Street North
Largo, FL 33773
(727) 538-2878
Fax: (727) 531-2739
Web site:
www.sunshinecrafts.com

specific items

General Beads:
Beadworks
149 Water Street
Norwalk, CT 06854
(203) 852-9108
Fax: (203) 855-8015
Web site:
www.beadworks.com

Toho Shoji, Inc.
990 Avenue of the Americas
New York, NY 10018
(212) 868-7465
Fax: (212) 868-7464

**Faceted beads and rhine-
stones in acrylic and glass:**
Enterprise Art
2860 Roosevelt Boulevard
Clearwater, FL 34620
(727) 531-7533
Catalog: (800) 366-2218
Fax: (800) 366-6121
www.EnterpriseArt.com

charms and jewelry findings:

Metalliferous
34 W. 46th Street
New York, NY 10036
(212) 944-0909
Fax: (212) 944-0644

glitter

Jones Tones
33865 United Avenue
Pueblo, CO 81001
(800) 397-9667

wire

Bullion in silver and gold:
Packaging Specialties
515 S. Michigan Avenue
Seattle, WA 98108
(206) 762-0540

Index

Page references in italics refer to photographs.